D1808546

THE SECURITY COUNCIL
WORKING METHODS HANDBOOK

The Security Council
Working Methods Handbook

Published by the United Nations
New York, New York 10017, United States of America
in cooperation with the Permanent Mission of Japan to the United Nations

Copyright © 2012 United Nations
All rights reserved

All queries on rights and licenses, including subsidiary rights, should be addressed to: United Nations Publications, 300 East 42nd Street, New York, New York 10017, United States of America; e-mail: *publications@un.org*; website: *un.org/publications*. Requests to reproduce excerpts should be addressed to: *permissions@un.org*.

ISBN: 978-92-1-137035-5
eISBN: 978-92-1-055117-5
United Nations Publication
Sales No. E.11.VII.1

Cover design: Graphic Design Unit, United Nations, New York

TABLE OF CONTENTS

INTRODUCTION

On the morning of 27 June 2011, 15 Security Council members seated in the Council Chamber raised their hands in unison to unanimously adopt resolution 1990 (2011) establishing a new mission, the "United Nations Interim Security Force for Abyei" (UNISFA), in order to quickly stabilize the situation in the critical border area of the Sudan in light of an agreement signed by the Government of the Sudan and the Sudan People's Liberation Movement of South Sudan only days before. Those observing the meeting would have seen that it lasted only five minutes, from 10:40 to 10:45 a.m. Consequently, they might have concluded that adopting such a resolution was a simple matter.

What these observers might have missed, however, were the essential working methods and procedures which guided the members of the Security Council from the moment they first took note of the deterioration of the situation in the Abyei area to their decision to act. During this time, the Council members decided to request both written information from the Secretariat and an oral briefing from a high-ranking official of the Department of Peacekeeping Operations; decided that they would listen to this briefing and respond to it in the format of "closed consultations of the whole" in their specially-designated Consultations Room; pored over a draft resolution proposed by the "lead country" and suggested improvements to the text; prepared the final draft of the resolution for adoption by requesting its translation beforehand into all six official languages of the United Nations; followed the customary practice for announcing the convening of the meeting in the Journal of the United Nations; and finally, after adopting the established agenda formulated for considering matters relating to the Sudan, followed the rules of procedure relating to the conduct of a vote in the Council.

This single example shows that having a range of working methods and procedures available to it is critical in enabling the Security Council to carry out its mandate according to the Charter of the United Nations, and make decisions that ensure prompt and effective action towards the maintenance of international peace and security. At the same time, when such decisions are made by the Security Council, having appropriate working methods and procedures is important in order to ensure the support of the wider United Nations membership.

The Security Council is perhaps best known to the general public as the principal organ responsible under the Charter of the United Nations for the maintenance of international peace and security. In carrying out this critically important mandate, the Security Council, which according to the Charter must be able to meet at any time if circumstances so require, has adopted over 2,000 resolutions relating to conflict and post-conflict situations around the globe. Since 1946, the Council has mandated the deployment of over 60 peacekeeping missions, and current missions are served by nearly 100,000 uniformed personnel. These peacekeeping missions have played an important role in maintaining lines of separation between combatants, facilitating peace agreements, and the protection of civilians. The Security Council has also developed and refined the use of non-military measures including arms embargoes, travel bans, and restrictions to guard against the exploitation of natural resources to fuel conflicts, as well as taking a lead role in the coordination of international counter-terrorism efforts.

The Security Council consists of five permanent members (China, France, the Russian Federation, the United Kingdom and the United States) and ten non-permanent members who are elected from among the Member States of the United Nations for a two-year term. The United Nations General Assembly holds elections each year, customarily in October, for the five non-permanent members which join the Council the following January as the five outgoing non-permanent members finish their two-year terms at the end of December.

Article 30 of the Charter stipulates that the Security Council shall adopt its own rules of procedure, and in 1946 the Council adopted its Provisional Rules of Procedure (S/96). Subsequently the Provisional Rules of Procedure were modified on several occasions; the last revision was made in 1982 (S/96/Rev.7) in order to add Arabic as the sixth official language, in conformity with General Assembly resolution 35/219 of 17 December 1980.

The Security Council has continued over time to improve its working methods, and to adapt them to changing realities both within the Council itself, and in the wider international context. To keep up with these changing realities, the members of the Council periodically have taken decisions to supplement the Provisional Rules of Procedure of the Security Council through adopting and publishing specific new working methods. Most commonly, the Security Council did so through the adoption of "Notes of the President of the Security Council", which put into writing practices and agreed measures among Council members to serve as guidance for the Council's work. These Notes by the President helped clarify the working methods for both Council members and the broader membership of the United Nations. The working methods they set out were intended to enhance the efficiency of the Security Council's work and make its activities more transparent, as well as to improve interaction and dialogue with non-Council members. Improvements in the working methods have also been considered one of the important issues for Security Council reform.

The Security Council Informal Working Group on Documentation and Other Procedural Questions (IWG) is the main forum where the "Notes" have been discussed and decided on by members of the Council. The Working Group was established in June 1993 to enhance and streamline ways and means whereby the Security Council addresses issues related to its documentation and other procedural questions. The Working Group meets as agreed by members of the Council and makes recommendations, proposals and suggestions to the members of the Council concerning the Council's documentation and other procedural questions.

In 2006, the Security Council decided that the Chair of the Informal Working Group on Documentation and Other Procedural Questions should serve on an annual basis, whereas previously the Informal Working Group had been chaired by each month's rotating Council President[1]. Under the Chairmanship of Japan, the Informal Working Group undertook to consolidate previous Notes by the President regarding Council practices into a comprehensive Note by the President (S/2006/507), which also contained additional new working methods of the Security Council. Member States referred to it as "Note 507". Following its adoption, Japan put together a handbook of documents relevant to the Security Council's working methods, including the Note 507, the Provisional Rules of Procedure and some background information on Council meetings, which was

---

[1] The President of the Security Council rotates on a monthly basis and follows the alphabetical names of Member States in the English language.

distributed to Member States. This 2006 handbook became known as the "Blue Book".

The Council's working methods continued to evolve. In 2010, again with Japan as the Chair, the Informal Working Group on Documentation and Other Procedural Questions undertook the task of updating Note 507 to reflect current practices of the Council and to reach agreement on additional working methods. The result was the adoption by the Security Council of a new Note by the President (S/2010/507). This Note incorporated recent practices such as greater interaction with troop-contributing countries to United Nations peacekeeping operations, the Peacebuilding Commission and the parties to a conflict. It also, for the first time, set out practices relating to the planning and conduct of Security Council missions. These are measures that have helped to make the work of the Security Council more effective and also more transparent. Subsequently, Japan issued a new handbook to include the revised Note 507, the Provisional Rules of Procedure, background information on Council meeting formats such as Informal Dialogues, as well as updated tables on rules for attendance of meetings and documentation. This new 2010 handbook has been referred to by some Member States as the "Green Book".

The present publication is based on the handbook issued by Japan. In addition to its usefulness to delegates of Member States and the broader United Nations community, this publication is also intended to serve as a guide for those in the general public who are interested in the United Nations and seek to learn more about how the Security Council operates. It reproduces a selection of relevant Articles of the UN Charter, in order for readers to understand the critically important mandate for the maintenance of international peace and security which the founders of the Organization accorded to the Security Council and which it continues to carry out today. Furthermore, the introduction and glossary will make it easier to understand for those who are not completely familiar with the Security Council and its context. This publication provides a wider readership with access to the same documents that diplomats utilize when familiarizing themselves with the Council's various meeting formats, rules and practices. This hopefully will further contribute to the understanding of the Security Council and its work.

NOTE BY THE PRESIDENT
OF THE SECURITY COUNCIL (S/2010/507)

1. In efforts to enhance the efficiency and transparency of the Council's work, as well as interaction and dialogue with non-Council members, the members of the Security Council are committed to implementing the measures described in the annex to the present note.

2. The annex is intended to be a concise and user-friendly list of the recent practices and newly agreed measures, which will serve as guidance for the Council's work. In this regard, some existing measures are recollected herein for the convenience of users.

3. The present note incorporates and further develops the notes by the President of the Security Council of 19 July 2006 (S/2006/507), 19 December 2007 (S/2007/749) and 31 December 2008 (S/2008/847), by superseding those notes.

4. For issues not mentioned in the present note, working methods regarding sanctions committees will continue to be governed by the working methods as adopted by individual sanctions committees and the notes and statements by the President of the Security Council listed in the note by the President of the Security Council of 7 February 2006 (S/2006/78). For issues not mentioned in the present note, working methods regarding interaction with troop- and police-contributing countries will continue to be governed by Security Council resolution 1353 (2001).

5. The members of the Council will continue their consideration of the Council's documentation and other procedural questions in the Informal Working Group on Docu-

mentation and Other Procedural Questions and other subsidiary bodies of the Council. The present note covers only the work done by the above-mentioned Working Group.

Annex
Contents

I. Agenda

1. The provisional agenda for formal meetings of the Council should be included in the *Journal of the United Nations* provided that it has been approved in informal consultations.

2. The members of the Council recall the desirability, whenever possible, of using descriptive formulations of agenda items at the time of their initial adoption to avoid having a number of separate agenda items on the same subject. When such a descriptive formulation exists, consideration may be given to subsuming earlier agenda items on the same subject under the descriptive formulation.

II. Briefings

3. The members of the Security Council agree that the President of the Council or his or her designate should provide substantive and detailed briefings to Member States in a timely manner. Such briefings should take place shortly after informal consultations of the whole. The members of the Security Council encourage the President of the Council to provide the attending Member States with copies of statements that he or she makes to the media following the informal consultations, if appropriate.

4. The members of the Security Council encourage the President of the Council to hold an informal briefing on the programme of work open to all Member States, after its adoption by the Council.

5. The members of the Security Council invite Chairs of the subsidiary bodies of the Security Council or their designates to give, on a regular basis, informal briefings, when

appropriate, on their activities to interested Member States. The members of the Security Council agree that the time and place of such briefings should be published in the *Journal of the United Nations.*

6. The members of the Security Council intend to continue to consider requesting the Secretariat to give an ad hoc briefing at Security Council meetings in cases in which an emergent situation which justifies a briefing arises.

7. The members of the Security Council intend to request the Secretariat to give ad hoc briefings at informal consultations on a daily basis, if necessary, when a situation justifies such briefings.

8. The members of the Security Council invite the Secretariat to continue its practice of circulating the briefing texts at "briefings".

9. The members of the Security Council invite the Secretariat, as a general rule, to provide a printed fact sheet, presentation materials and/or any other relevant reference materials, whenever possible, to Council members on the day prior to the consultations, when briefings in the Security Council consultations room are not given on the basis of a written report.

III. Documentation

10. The members of the Security Council intend to intensify their efforts to publicize decisions and other relevant information of the Council and its subsidiary bodies to the Member States and other organizations through correspondence, websites, outreach activities and other means, when appropriate. The members of the Security Council intend to continue to examine ways to enhance its activi-

ties in this regard. The members of the Security Council encourage subsidiary bodies of the Council to continue to review periodically policies concerning access to their documents, as appropriate.

11. The members of the Security Council agree that reports of the Secretary-General should be circulated to Council members and made available in all official languages of the United Nations at least four working days before the Council is scheduled to consider them. The members of the Security Council also agree that the same rule should apply to making such reports available to relevant participants in Council meetings at which those reports are discussed, including the distribution of the reports on peacekeeping missions to all participants in meetings of troop- and police-contributing countries.

12. The members of the Security Council agree to consider setting a six-month interval as the standard reporting period, unless the situation provides reason for shorter or longer intervals. The members of the Security Council also agree to define reporting intervals as clearly as possible when adopting resolutions. The members of the Security Council further agree to request oral reporting, which does not require submission of a written report, if the members of the Council consider that it would serve the purpose satisfactorily, and to indicate that request as clearly as possible.

13. The members of the Security Council encourage the Secretary-General to include a section in his reports where all recommendations are listed, when presenting recommendations to the Council regarding the mandate of a United Nations mission.

14. The members of the Security Council encourage the Secretary-General to make reports as concise as possible and give an ample cut-off time in order for the reports to be issued in a timely manner. The Secretariat is encouraged to supplement and update information contained in reports of the Secretary-General by including information about the most recent developments during briefings.

15. The members of the Security Council intend to request the Secretary-General to include policy recommendations on long-term strategy in his reports, if appropriate.

16. Reports of the Secretary-General will specify the date on which the document is physically and electronically distributed in addition to the date of signature by the Secretary-General.

17. The Security Council agrees to cooperate with other organs of the United Nations in synchronizing reporting obligations of the Secretariat on the same subject, if appropriate, while giving priority to the effective work of the Council.

18. The members of the Security Council request the Secretariat to update the Council towards the end of each month on the progress in the preparation of the reports of the Secretary-General to be issued the following month. The members of the Security Council also request the Secretariat to communicate with the Council immediately if it expects reports to be delayed beyond their deadlines or if reports that have not been requested by the Council are expected to be issued.

19. The members of the Security Council encourage the Secretariat to ensure that all information provided to

Council members is transmitted electronically, including by fax.

IV. Informal consultations

20. The members of the Security Council encourage the President of the Council to suggest, through consultations with interested members and/or the Secretariat, as appropriate, a few areas for Council members and the Secretariat to focus on at the Council's next informal consultations, without the intention of prescribing the scope of discussion, at least one day before the consultations are to be held.

21. The members of the Security Council agree that when briefings are being provided to the Council members by senior Secretariat officials, the number of staff members accompanying those officials in the consultations should be kept to a strict minimum. Unless otherwise decided, the Secretariat staff from offices other than those of the designated briefer or from United Nations agencies will normally not be invited to attend consultations. Unless otherwise decided, the Security Council Affairs Division of the Department of Political Affairs will be responsible for keeping the Office of the Spokesperson for the Secretary-General informed of matters which may require its action.

22. As a general rule, the purpose of initial remarks or ad hoc briefings delivered by members of the Secretariat is to supplement and update written reports of the Secretary-General or to provide members of the Council with more specific on-the-ground information on the most recent developments, which may not be covered in the written report. The members of the Security Council encourage members of the Secretariat to focus on key issues and to provide the latest information, as necessary, without re-

peating the content of written reports already available to members of the Council.

23. The members of the Security Council intend, where they agree with a previous speaker, in part or in whole, to express that agreement without repeating the same content.

24. The members of the Security Council agree that, as a general rule, the President of the Council should adhere to the prescribed speakers' list. The members of the Security Council encourage the President to facilitate interaction by inviting any participant in the consultations to speak at any time, irrespective of the order of the prescribed speakers' list, when the discussion requires it.

25. The members of the Security Council encourage speakers to direct their questions not only to the Secretariat, but also to other members.

26. The members of the Security Council do not discourage each other from taking the floor more than once, in the interest of making consultations more interactive.

27. The members of the Security Council invite the Secretariat to continue its practice of circulating all press statements issued by the Secretary-General or by the Secretary-General's spokesperson in connection with matters of concern to the Security Council.

V. Meetings

Conduct of meetings

28. In order to increase the transparency of its work, the Security Council reaffirms its commitment to increase re-

course to open meetings, particularly at the early stage in its consideration of a matter.

29. The Security Council encourages, as a general rule, all participants, both members and non-members of the Council, in Council meetings to deliver their statements in five minutes or less. The Security Council also encourages each briefer to limit initial remarks to 15 minutes, unless otherwise decided by the Council.

30. The Security Council encourages participants in Council meetings to express agreement without repeating the same content, if they agree, in part or in whole, with the content of a previous statement.

31. The Security Council agrees that, when non-members are invited to speak to the Council, those who have a direct interest in the outcome of the matter under consideration may speak prior to Council members, if appropriate.

32. In line with paragraph 170 (a) of the 2005 World Summit Outcome (General Assembly resolution 60/1) and Security Council resolution 1631 (2005), the members of the Security Council agree to continue to expand consultation and cooperation with regional and subregional organizations, including by inviting relevant organizations to participate in the Council's public and private meetings, when appropriate.

33. In order to further encourage substantive discussions with troop- and police- contributing countries, in accordance with Security Council resolution 1353 (2001), the members of the Security Council encourage the attendance of appropriate military and political officers from each participating mission at meetings with troop-contributing

countries. The members of the Security Council emphasize the importance of consulting with troop- and police-contributing countries, including holding meetings, preferably, one week before the Security Council considers mandate renewals or modifications. The members of the Security Council encourage the President of the Council to provide sufficient time for the meetings and to provide to the other members of the Council a summary of the meetings with troop- and police-contributing countries that are held before the Council discusses mandate renewals or modifications.

34. When non-members of the Security Council are invited to speak at its meetings, they will be seated at the Council table on alternate sides of the President, the first speaker being seated on the President's right.

Notification

35. The members of the Security Council invite the Secretariat to notify Member States of unscheduled or emergency meetings not only by e-mail but also through the Council website and by telephone as necessary.

Format

36. In an effort further to advance the resolution of a matter under consideration, the members of the Security Council agree to use a range of meeting options from which they can select the one best suited to facilitate specific discussions. Recognizing that the provisional rules of procedure of the Security Council and their own practice provide them with considerable flexibility in choosing how best to structure their meetings, members of the Council agree that meetings of the Council could be structured according to, but not limited to, the following formats:

(a) Public meetings

(i) Functions

To take action and/or hold, inter alia, briefings and debates.

(ii) Presence and participation

The presence and participation of non-Council members in public meetings should be in accordance with the provisional rules of procedure. The Council's practice, as described below, is understood as being in accordance with the provisional rules of procedure, although it should not under any circumstances be understood as replacing or substituting for the provisional rules of procedure:

a. Any Member of the United Nations that is not a member of the Security Council may be present at its delegation's designated seats in the Council Chamber;

b. On a case-by-case basis, any Member of the United Nations that is not a member of the Security Council, members of the Secretariat and other persons may be invited to participate in the discussion, including for the purpose of giving briefings to the Council, in accordance with rule 37 or 39 of the provisional rules of procedure.

(iii) Descriptions in the provisional monthly programme of work

The members of the Security Council intend to continue to include the following formats for public meetings in the provisional monthly programme of work (calendar) when they plan to adopt, in general, the corresponding procedures:

a. "Open debate": briefings may or may not be conducted, and Council members may deliver statements; non-Council members may also be invited to participate in the discussion upon their request;

b. "Debate": briefings may be conducted, and Council members may deliver statements; non-Council members that are directly concerned or affected or have a special interest in the matter under consideration may be invited to participate in the discussion upon their request;

c. "Briefing": briefings are conducted, and only Council members may deliver statements following briefings;

d. "Adoption": Council members may or may not deliver statements before and/or after adopting, inter alia, resolutions and presidential statements; non-Council members may or may not be invited to participate in the discussion upon their request.

(b) Private meetings

(i) Functions

To conduct discussion and/or take actions, for example, recommendation regarding the appointment of the Secretary-General, without the attendance of the public or the press.

(ii) Presence and participation

The presence and participation of non-Council members in private meetings should be in accordance with the provisional rules of procedure. The Council's practice, as described below, is understood as being in accordance with the provisional rules of procedure, although it should not under any circumstances be understood as replacing or substituting for the provisional rules of procedure:

On a case-by-case basis, any Member of the United Nations which is not a member of the Security Council, members of the Secretariat and other persons may be invited to be present or to participate in the discussion, including for the purpose of giving briefings to the Council, in accordance with rule 37 or 39 of the provisional rules of procedure.

(iii) Descriptions in the provisional monthly programme of work

The members of the Security Council intend to continue to include the following formats for private meetings in the provisional monthly programme of work (calendar) when they plan to adopt, in general, the corresponding procedures:

a.   "Private meeting": briefings or debates may be conducted, and Council members may deliver statements; any Member of the United Nations which is not a member of the Security Council, members of the Secretariat and other persons may be invited to be present or to participate in the discussion, upon their request, in accordance with rule 37 or 39 of the provisional rules of procedure;

b.   "TCC meeting": briefings may be conducted, and Council members may deliver statements; parties described in resolution 1353 (2001) are invited to participate in the discussion, in accordance with the resolution.

Distribution of statements

37. Texts of statements made at the meetings of the Security Council will, at the request of the delegation making the statement, be distributed by the Secretariat inside the Council Chamber to Council members and other Member States and permanent observers to the United Nations present at the meeting. A delegation requesting the distribution of its statement is encouraged to provide a sufficient number of copies (200) to the Secretariat in advance of the statement. When a delegation does not provide to the Secretariat a sufficient number of copies of its statement, those copies will be placed outside the Council Chamber at the end of the meeting. Delegations are requested not to make statements otherwise available during the meeting.

VI. Programme of work

38. The members of the Security Council encourage the President of the Council to publish a streamlined tentative monthly forecast of the programme of work on the Council website as soon as it has been distributed to Council members.

39. The forecast should be made available in all official languages "for information only/not an official document", and there should be a cover note which reads: "This tentative forecast of the programme of work of the Security Council has been prepared by the Secretariat for the President of the Council. The forecast covers in particular those matters that may be taken up during the month pursuant to earlier decisions of the Council. The fact that a matter is or is not included in the forecast carries no implication that it will or will not be taken up during the month: the actual programme of work will be determined by developments and the views of members of the Council."

40. The members of the Council have agreed that the following reminder should be placed in the *Journal of the United Nations* each month: "The monthly tentative forecast has been made available at the website of the Security Council, in accordance with the note by the President of the Security Council dated 26 July 2010 (S/2010/507). Copies of the tentative forecast have also been placed in the delegations' boxes and may be collected at the delegations' pick-up areas as of [date]."

41. The members of the Security Council agree that the President of the Council should update the provisional monthly programme of work (calendar) and make it available to the public through the Council website each time it is revised and distributed to Council members, with appropriate indication of the revised items.

VII. Resolutions and presidential statements

42. The members of the Security Council reaffirm that all members of the Security Council should be allowed to participate fully in the preparation of, inter alia, the resolutions, presidential statements and press statements of the Council. The members of the Security Council also reaffirm that the drafting of all documents such as resolutions and presidential statements as well as press statements should be carried out in a manner that will allow adequate participation of all members of the Council.

43. The members of the Security Council intend to continue to informally consult with the broader United Nations membership, in particular interested Member States, including countries directly involved or specifically affected, neighbouring States and countries with particular contributions to make, as well as with regional organizations and Groups of Friends, when drafting, inter alia,

resolutions, presidential statements and press statements, as appropriate.

44. The members of the Security Council agree to consider making draft resolutions and presidential statements as well as other draft documents available as appropriate to non-members of the Council as soon as such documents are introduced within informal consultations of the whole, or earlier, if so authorized by the authors of the draft document.

45. The President of the Security Council should, when so requested by the Council members, and without prejudice to his or her responsibilities as President, draw the attention of the representative(s) of the Member State(s), regional organizations and arrangements concerned to relevant statements to the press made by the President on behalf of Council members or decisions of the Council. The Secretariat should also continue to bring to the knowledge of those concerned, including non-State actors, through the relevant Special Representatives, Representatives and Envoys of the Secretary-General and United Nations Resident Coordinators, resolutions and presidential statements of the Security Council as well as statements to the press made by the President of the Council on behalf of the Council members, and ensure their promptest communication and widest possible dissemination. The Secretariat should further issue, as United Nations press releases, all written statements to the press made by the President of the Security Council on behalf of Council members, upon clearance by the President.

VIII. Subsidiary bodies

46. The members of the Security Council encourage the Chairs of all subsidiary bodies to continue to report to the

Council on any outstanding issues, when necessary and in any event on a regular basis, in order to receive strategic guidance from the Council.

47. The members of the Security Council encourage subsidiary bodies of the Council to seek the views of Member States with strong interest in their areas of work. The members of the Security Council in particular encourage sanctions committees to seek the views of Member States that are particularly affected by the sanctions.

48. The members of the Security Council encourage the Secretariat to provide administrative and substantive support to the subsidiary bodies of the Security Council.

49. The members of the Security Council encourage Chairs of the subsidiary bodies of the Council to make the schedules of meetings of subsidiary bodies available to the public, when appropriate, through their websites and the *Journal of the United Nations.*

50. The members of the Security Council welcome the participation in the meetings of the Security Council Working Group on Peacekeeping Operations of the Secretariat, troop- and police-contributing countries and other major stakeholders, and encourage this practice in order to foster closer cooperation between the Council and those actors.

IX. Matters of which the Council is seized

51. Rule 11 of the provisional rules of procedure of the Security Council provides that the Secretary-General shall communicate each week to the representatives on the Security Council a summary statement of matters

of which the Security Council is seized and of the stage reached in their consideration.

52. The practice of including an agenda item in the summary statement once it has been adopted at a formal meeting of the Security Council will remain unchanged.

53. At the beginning of each year, the Security Council will review the summary statement in order to determine if the Council has concluded its consideration of any of the listed items, in particular those items that were considered for the first time during the preceding year, and whether, consequently, such items should be deleted from the statement. Further, except as herein provided, any item which has not been considered by the Security Council during the preceding three calendar years will also be deleted.

54. The preliminary annual summary statement issued in January of each year by the Secretary-General on matters of which the Council is seized will identify the items to be deleted from the list. The first summary statement issued in March of each year will reflect the deletion of those items, unless a State Member of the United Nations notifies the President of the Security Council by the end of February of that year that it requests an item to remain on the summary statement, in which case such item will remain on the statement for one year, unless the Security Council decides otherwise.

55. The deletion of an item does not imply that such an item cannot be taken up by the Security Council as and when it deems necessary in the future.

56. The summary statement will be presented in the format of two sections, as follows: one section comprising items which have been considered by the Security Council at a meeting during the preceding three-year period, and another section comprising items which have not been considered at a meeting during the preceding three-year period but which the Security Council has decided to retain at the request of a Member State.

57. The Security Council reconfirms that the first summary statement of each month will contain a full, updated list of items of which the Security Council is seized. For intervening weeks, a weekly addendum to the summary statement will be issued listing only those items on which further action has been taken by the Council during the previous week or indicating that there has been no change during that period.

58. The Security Council reconfirms that references given for each item listed in the summary statement will be the dates when the item was first taken up by the Council at a formal meeting and the most recent formal meeting of the Council held on that item.

X. Communication with the Secretariat and outside

59. The members of the Security Council intend to seek the views of Member States that are parties to a conflict and/or other interested and affected parties. For that purpose, the Security Council may, inter alia, utilize private meetings when public meetings are not appropriate, in which case invitations are also to be extended in accordance with rules 37 and 39 of the Council's provisional rules of procedure. The Security Council, when it deems appropriate, may also utilize informal dialogues.

60. The members of the Security Council intend to continue to maintain regular communication with the General Assembly and the Economic and Social Council for better coordination among the principal organs of the United Nations. To that end, the members of the Security Council encourage the President of the Council to continue holding meetings with the Presidents of the General Assembly and the Economic and Social Council on a regular basis.

61. The members of the Security Council also intend to maintain regular communication with the Peacebuilding Commission. As appropriate, the members of the Council intend to invite the Chairs of country-specific configurations of the Peacebuilding Commission to participate in formal Security Council meetings at which the situation concerning the country in question is considered, or on a case-by-case basis, for an exchange of views in an informal dialogue.

62. The members of the Security Council are encouraged to prepare a monthly assessment of their presidency in a timely manner, which can be utilized by the member of the Council preparing the annual report.

63. The members of the Security Council intend to make the best use of all mechanisms available, as appropriate, to convey policy guidance to the Secretary-General, including dialogue, letters from the President, adoption of resolutions or presidential statements, or any other means deemed appropriate.

64. The members of the Security Council, through the Secretary-General, invite new Special Representatives of the Secretary-General to engage in dialogue with members of the Council before assuming their duties under new man-

dates, including in the field, in order to obtain Council members' views on the objectives and the mandates.

65. The members of the Security Council intend to utilize "Arria-formula" meetings as a flexible and informal forum for enhancing their deliberations. To that end, members of the Security Council may invite on an informal basis any Member State, relevant organization or individual to participate in "Arria-formula" informal meetings. The members of the Security Council agree to consider using such meetings to enhance their contact with civil society and non-governmental organizations, including local non-governmental organizations suggested by United Nations field offices. The members of the Security Council encourage the introduction of such measures as lengthening lead times, defining topics that participants might address and permitting their participation by video teleconference.

XI. Security Council missions

66. The members of the Security Council underline the value of Security Council missions for understanding and assessing particular conflicts or situations on the agenda of the Council. Security Council missions should be planned as early as practicable with the members of the Security Council that will be participating in the mission. Members of the Security Council will designate a member or members to coordinate a particular Security Council mission.

67. The designated member or members will draft terms of reference for the mission as early as possible in consultation with Security Council members and the Secretariat. The terms of reference should outline the dates of the mission, its purpose, the proposed agenda and the composition of the mission. The terms of

reference should be issued as a Security Council document.

68. The members of the Security Council encourage Security Council missions to continue to avoid restricting their meetings to those with governmental interlocutors and interlocutors of conflict parties and to hold, as appropriate, meetings with local civil society leaders, non-governmental organizations and other interested parties.

69. Upon the return of the mission, the designated member or members should brief the Security Council on the mission orally and/or with a written report which should be issued as a document of the Security Council.

XII. Annual report

70. The Security Council will take the necessary action to ensure the timely submission of its report to the General Assembly. For that purpose:

(a) The Security Council will continue with the existing practice whereby the annual report is submitted to the General Assembly in a single volume. The period of coverage for the reports shall be from 1 August of one year to 31 July of the next;

(b) The Secretariat should continue to submit the draft report to the members of the Council no later than 30 September, immediately following the period covered by the report, so that it may be discussed and thereafter adopted by the Council in time for consideration by the General

Assembly during the main part of the regular session of the General Assembly.

71. The report shall contain an introduction, to be prepared in accordance with the following guidelines:

(a)   The draft introduction to the report should continue to be prepared under the leadership and responsibility of the President of the Council for the month of July of each calendar year and should continue to be approved by all current members of the Council and the immediate past elected members who served on the Council during the reporting period covered;

(b)   While drafting the introduction to the report, the President for the month of July may, when necessary, seek advice from other members of the Council;

(c)   The introduction to the report should contain concise information about the nature of all decisions taken by the Council during the period covered, in particular all resolutions and presidential statements;

(d)   The member of the Council preparing the introduction is encouraged to consult for reference the monthly assessments described in paragraph 62 above.

72. The remainder of the report shall be prepared by the Secretariat and shall be approved by all current members of the Council and the immediate past elected members who served on the Council during the reporting period covered, and shall contain the following parts:

(a)   Part I shall contain a brief statistical description of the key activities relating to all questions considered by the Security Council under its responsibility for the maintenance of international peace and security during the period covered by the report, including a list of each of the following with document symbols, as appropriate:

    (i)   All decisions, resolutions, presidential statements and official communiqués adopted by the Security Council;

    (ii)   Meetings of the Security Council, including with troop- and police-contributing countries;

    (iii)   Meetings of subsidiary bodies, including counter-terrorism committees, sanctions committees and working groups;

    (iv)   Reports of panels and monitoring mechanisms;

    (v)   Reports of Security Council missions undertaken;

    (vi)   (vi) Peacekeeping operations established, functioning or terminated;

    (vii)   Assistance missions and offices established, functioning or terminated;

    (viii)   Reports of the Secretary-General submitted to the Security Council;

    (ix)   References to the summary statements by the Secretary-General on matters of which the Security Council was seized for the period covered by the report;

(x) Notes by the President of the Security Council and other documents issued by the Security Council for the further improvement of the work of the Council;

(xi) Assessment reports issued by the individual monthly presidencies of the Council on its work;

(b) Part II shall contain information relating to each question considered by the Security Council during the reporting period, in at least one formal meeting, under its responsibility for the maintenance of international peace and security:

(i) Factual data on the number of meetings and informal consultations;

(ii) A notice of all decisions, resolutions, presidential statements, and draft resolutions considered by the Council at its meetings but not adopted;

(iii) A list of the peacekeeping operations and assistance missions and offices established, functioning or terminated, as appropriate;

(iv) A list of the relevant panels and monitoring mechanisms and their reports, as appropriate;

(v) A list of the reports of the Secretary-General submitted to the Security Council;

(vi) A list of the Security Council missions undertaken and their reports, as appropriate;

(vii) All communications issued by the Council or transmitted to the Council in connection with each agenda item considered;

(c)   Part III shall contain an account of the other matters considered by the Security Council;

(d)   Part IV shall contain an account of the work of the Military Staff Committee;

(e)   Part V shall cover matters that were brought to the attention of the Council but not discussed at the meetings of the Council during the reporting period;

(f)   The members of the Security Council acknowledge that the work of the Security Council subsidiary bodies is an inseparable part of the Council's work. Part VI of the report shall therefore contain concise information about the work of subsidiary bodies of the Security Council, including counter-terrorism committees, sanctions committees, working groups, and international tribunals established by the Security Council, as appropriate.

73. The Secretariat should post the current annual report of the Security Council on the United Nations website. The relevant web page should be updated to provide the information as necessitated under future notes issued by the President of the Security Council with respect to the annual report.

74. The report will continue to be adopted at a public meeting of the Security Council where members of the Council who wish to do so may comment on the work of the Council for the period covered by the report. The President of the Council for the month in which the report is submitted to the General Assembly will also make reference to the verbatim record of the Council's discussion prior to its adoption of the annual report.

75. If appropriate, the President of the Security Council will continue the practice of not scheduling meetings or informal consultations of the Council on the first day of the debate on the report in the General Assembly.

XIII. Newly elected members

76. The Security Council invites the newly elected members of the Council to attend all meetings of the Council and its subsidiary bodies and the informal consultations of the whole, for a period of six weeks immediately preceding their term of membership or as soon as they have been elected, if the election is held less than six weeks prior to the beginning of their terms. The Security Council also invites the Secretariat to provide all relevant communications of the Council to the newly elected members during the above-mentioned period.

77. The members of the Security Council also agree that, if an incoming member will be assuming the presidency of the Council in the first two months of its term on the Council, it will be invited to attend the informal consultations of the whole for the period of two months immediately preceding its term of membership (that is, with effect from 1 November).

78. The Security Council invites the Secretariat to continue to take appropriate measures to familiarize the newly elected members with the work of the Council and its subsidiary bodies, including by providing briefing materials and holding seminars before they begin to attend Council meetings.

ANNEXES

Annex 1:
Selected Articles of the UN Charter related to the Security Council

Preamble

WE THE PEOPLES OF THE UNITED NATIONS DETERMINED

- to save succeeding generations from the scourge of war, which twice in our lifetime has brought untold sorrow to mankind, and

- to reaffirm faith in fundamental human rights, in the dignity and worth of the human person, in the equal rights of men and women and of nations large and small, and

- to establish conditions under which justice and respect for the obligations arising from treaties and other sources of international law can be maintained, and

- to promote social progress and better standards of life in larger freedom,

AND FOR THESE ENDS

- to practice tolerance and live together in peace with one another as good neighbours, and

- to unite our strength to maintain international peace and security, and

- to ensure, by the acceptance of principles and the institution of methods, that armed force shall not be used, save in the common interest, and

- to employ international machinery for the promotion of the economic and social advancement of all peoples,

HAVE RESOLVED TO COMBINE OUR EFFORTS TO ACCOMPLISH THESE AIMS

Accordingly, our respective Governments, through representatives assembled in the city of San Francisco, who have exhibited their full powers found to be in good and due form, have agreed to the present Charter of the United Nations and do hereby establish an international organization to be known as the United Nations.

Chapter I:
Purposes and Principles

Article 1

The Purposes of the United Nations are:

1. To maintain international peace and security, and to that end: to take effective collective measures for the prevention and removal of threats to the peace, and for the suppression of acts of aggression or other breaches of the peace, and to bring about by peaceful means, and in conformity with the principles of justice and international law, adjustment or settlement of international disputes or situations which might lead to a breach of the peace;

2. To develop friendly relations among nations based on respect for the principle of equal rights and self-determination of peoples, and to take other appropriate measures to strengthen universal peace;

3. To achieve international co-operation in solving international problems of an economic, social, cultural, or humanitarian character, and in promoting and encouraging respect for human rights and for fundamental freedoms for all without distinction as to race, sex, language, or religion; and

4. To be a centre for harmonizing the actions of nations in the attainment of these common ends.

Article 2

The Organization and its Members, in pursuit of the Purposes stated in Article 1, shall act in accordance with the following Principles.

1. The Organization is based on the principle of the sovereign equality of all its Members.

2. All Members, in order to ensure to all of them the rights and benefits resulting from membership, shall fulfill in good faith the obligations assumed by them in accordance with the present Charter.

3. All Members shall settle their international disputes by peaceful means in such a manner that international peace and security, and justice, are not endangered.

4.   All Members shall refrain in their international rela-
      tions from the threat or use of force against the terri-
      torial integrity or political independence of any state,
      or in any other manner inconsistent with the Pur-
      poses of the United Nations.

5.   All Members shall give the United Nations every as-
      sistance in any action it takes in accordance with the
      present Charter, and shall refrain from giving assis-
      tance to any state against which the United Nations is
      taking preventive or enforcement action.

6.   The Organization shall ensure that states which are
      not Members of the United Nations act in accordance
      with these Principles so far as may be necessary for
      the maintenance of international peace and security.

7.   Nothing contained in the present Charter shall au-
      thorize the United Nations to intervene in matters
      which are essentially within the domestic jurisdiction
      of any state or shall require the Members to submit
      such matters to settlement under the present Char-
      ter; but this principle shall not prejudice the applica-
      tion of enforcement measures under Chapter Vll.

Chapter II:
Membership

[…]

Article 4

1.   Membership in the United Nations is open to all other
      peace-loving states which accept the obligations con-
      tained in the present Charter and, in the judgment of

the Organization, are able and willing to carry out these obligations.

2.   The admission of any such state to membership in the United Nations will be effected by a decision of the General Assembly upon the recommendation of the Security Council.

Article 5

A Member of the United Nations against which preventive or enforcement action has been taken by the Security Council may be suspended from the exercise of the rights and privileges of membership by the General Assembly upon the recommendation of the Security Council. The exercise of these rights and privileges may be restored by the Security Council.

Article 6

A Member of the United Nations which has persistently violated the Principles contained in the present Charter may be expelled from the Organization by the General Assembly upon the recommendation of the Security Council.

Chapter III:
Organs

Article 7

1.   There are established as principal organs of the United Nations: a General Assembly, a Security Council, an Economic and Social Council, a Trusteeship Council, an International Court of Justice and a Secretariat.

2.   Such subsidiary organs as may be found necessary may be established in accordance with the present Charter.

Article 8

The United Nations shall place no restrictions on the eligibility of men and women to participate in any capacity and under conditions of equality in its principal and subsidiary organs.

Chapter IV:
The General Assembly

[...]

Article 10

The General Assembly may discuss any questions or any matters within the scope of the present Charter or relating to the powers and functions of any organs provided for in the present Charter, and, except as provided in Article 12, may make recommendations to the Members of the United Nations or to the Security Council or to both on any such questions or matters.

Article 11

1.   The General Assembly may consider the general principles of co-operation in the maintenance of international peace and security, including the principles governing disarmament and the regulation of armaments, and may make recommendations with regard to such principles to the Members or to the Security Council or to both.

2.   The General Assembly may discuss any questions relating to the maintenance of international peace and security brought before it by any Member of the United Nations, or by the Security Council, or by a state which is not a Member of the United Nations in accordance with Article 35, paragraph 2, and, except as provided in Article 12, may make recommendations with regard to any such questions to the state or states concerned or to the Security Council or to both. Any such question on which action is necessary shall be referred to the Security Council by the General Assembly either before or after discussion.

3.   The General Assembly may call the attention of the Security Council to situations which are likely to endanger international peace and security.

4.   The powers of the General Assembly set forth in this Article shall not limit the general scope of Article 10.

Article 12

1.   While the Security Council is exercising in respect of any dispute or situation the functions assigned to it in the present Charter, the General Assembly shall not make any recommendation with regard to that dispute or situation unless the Security Council so requests.

2.   The Secretary-General, with the consent of the Security Council, shall notify the General Assembly at each session of any matters relative to the maintenance of international peace and security which are being dealt with by the Security Council and shall similarly notify the General Assembly, or the Members of the United Nations if the General Assembly is

not in session, immediately the Security Council ceases to deal with such matters. [...]

Article 15

1. The General Assembly shall receive and consider annual and special reports from the Security Council; these reports shall include an account of the measures that the Security Council has decided upon or taken to maintain international peace and security.

2. The General Assembly shall receive and consider reports from the other organs of the United Nations. [...]

Chapter V:
The Security Council

Article 23

1. The Security Council shall consist of fifteen Members of the United Nations. The Republic of China, France, the Union of Soviet Socialist Republics, the United Kingdom of Great Britain and Northern Ireland, and the United States of America shall be permanent members of the Security Council. The General Assembly shall elect ten other Members of the United Nations to be non-permanent members of the Security Council, due regard being specially paid, in the first instance to the contribution of Members of the United Nations to the maintenance of international peace and security and to the other purposes of the Organization, and also to equitable geographical distribution.

2. The non-permanent members of the Security Council shall be elected for a term of two years. In the first election of the non-permanent members after the increase of the membership of the Security Council from eleven to fifteen, two of the four additional members shall be chosen for a term of one year. A retiring member shall not be eligible for immediate re-election.

3. Each member of the Security Council shall have one representative.

Article 24

1. In order to ensure prompt and effective action by the United Nations, its Members confer on the Security Council primary responsibility for the maintenance of international peace and security, and agree that in carrying out its duties under this responsibility the Security Council acts on their behalf.

2. In discharging these duties the Security Council shall act in accordance with the Purposes and Principles of the United Nations. The specific powers granted to the Security Council for the discharge of these duties are laid down in Chapters VI, VII, VIII, and XII.

3. The Security Council shall submit annual and, when necessary, special reports to the General Assembly for its consideration.

Article 25

The Members of the United Nations agree to accept and carry out the decisions of the Security Council in accordance with the present Charter.

Article 26

In order to promote the establishment and maintenance of international peace and security with the least diversion for armaments of the world's human and economic resources, the Security Council shall be responsible for formulating, with the assistance of the Military Staff Committee referred to in Article 47, plans to be submitted to the Members of the United Nations for the establishment of a system for the regulation of armaments.

Article 27

1. Each member of the Security Council shall have one vote.

2. Decisions of the Security Council on procedural matters shall be made by an affirmative vote of nine members.

3. Decisions of the Security Council on all other matters shall be made by an affirmative vote of nine members including the concurring votes of the permanent members; provided that, in decisions under Chapter VI, and under paragraph 3 of Article 52, a party to a dispute shall abstain from voting.

Article 28

1. The Security Council shall be so organized as to be able to function continuously. Each member of the Security Council shall for this purpose be represented at all times at the seat of the Organization.

2. The Security Council shall hold periodic meetings at which each of its members may, if it so desires be

represented by a member of the government or by some other specially designated representative.

3.   The Security Council may hold meetings at such places other than the seat of the Organization as in its judgment will best facilitate its work.

Article 29

The Security Council may establish such subsidiary organs as it deems necessary for the performance of its functions.

Article 30

The Security Council shall adopt its own rules of procedure, including the method of selecting its President.

Article 31

Any Member of the United Nations which is not a member of the Security Council may participate, without vote, in the discussion of any question brought before the Security Council whenever the latter considers that the interests of that Member are specially affected.

Article 32

Any Member of the United Nations which is not a member of the Security Council or any state which is not a Member of the United Nations, if it is a party to a dispute under consideration by the Security Council, shall be invited to participate, without vote, in the discussion relating to the dispute. The Security Council shall lay down such conditions as it deems just for the participation of a state which is not a Member of the United Nations.

Chapter VI:
Pacific Settlement of Disputes

Article 33

1.   The parties to any dispute, the continuance of which is likely to endanger the maintenance of international peace and security, shall, first of all, seek a solution by negotiation, enquiry, mediation, conciliation, arbitration, judicial settlement, resort to regional agencies or arrangements, or other peaceful means of their own choice.

2.   The Security Council shall, when it deems necessary, call upon the parties to settle their dispute by such means.

Article 34

The Security Council may investigate any dispute, or any situation which might lead to international friction or give rise to a dispute, in order to determine whether the continuance of the dispute or situation is likely to endanger the maintenance of international peace and security.

Article 35

1.   Any Member of the United Nations may bring any dispute, or any situation of the nature referred to in Article 34, to the attention of the Security Council or of the General Assembly.

2.   A state which is not a Member of the United Nations may bring to the attention of the Security Council or of the General Assembly any dispute to which it is a party if it accepts in advance, for the purposes of the

dispute, the obligations of pacific settlement provided in the present Charter.

3.   The proceedings of the General Assembly in respect
of matters brought to its attention under this Article
will be subject to the provisions of Articles 11 and
12.

Article 36

1.   The Security Council may, at any stage of a dispute of
the nature referred to in Article 33 or of a situation
of like nature, recommend appropriate procedures or
methods of adjustment.

2.   The Security Council should take into consideration
any procedures for the settlement of the dispute
which have already been adopted by the parties.

3.   In making recommendations under this Article the
Security Council should also take into consideration
that legal disputes should as a general rule be referred by the parties to the International Court of
Justice in accordance with the provisions of the Statute of the Court.

Article 37

1.   Should the parties to a dispute of the nature referred
to in Article 33 fail to settle it by the means indicated
in that Article, they shall refer it to the Security
Council.

2.   If the Security Council deems that the continuance of
the dispute is in fact likely to endanger the maintenance of international peace and security, it shall decide whether to take action under Article 36 or to

recommend such terms of settlement as it may consider appropriate.

Article 38

Without prejudice to the provisions of Articles 33 to 37, the Security Council may, if all the parties to any dispute so request, make recommendations to the parties with a view to a pacific settlement of the dispute.

Chapter VII:
Action With Respect to Threats to the Peace, Breaches of the Peace, and Acts of Aggression

Article 39

The Security Council shall determine the existence of any threat to the peace, breach of the peace, or act of aggression and shall make recommendations, or decide what measures shall be taken in accordance with Articles 41 and 42, to maintain or restore international peace and security.

Article 40

In order to prevent an aggravation of the situation, the Security Council may, before making the recommendations or deciding upon the measures provided for in Article 39, call upon the parties concerned to comply with such provisional measures as it deems necessary or desirable. Such provisional measures shall be without prejudice to the rights, claims, or position of the parties concerned. The Security Council shall duly take account of failure to comply with such provisional measures.

Article 41

The Security Council may decide what measures not involving the use of armed force are to be employed to give effect to its decisions, and it may call upon the Members of the United Nations to apply such measures. These may include complete or partial interruption of economic relations and of rail, sea, air, postal, telegraphic, radio, and other means of communication, and the severance of diplomatic relations.

Article 42

Should the Security Council consider that measures provided for in Article 41 would be inadequate or have proved to be inadequate, it may take such action by air, sea, or land forces as may be necessary to maintain or restore international peace and security. Such action may include demonstrations, blockade, and other operations by air, sea, or land forces of Members of the United Nations.

Article 43

1. All Members of the United Nations, in order to contribute to the maintenance of international peace and security, undertake to make available to the Security Council, on its call and in accordance with a special agreement or agreements, armed forces, assistance, and facilities, including rights of passage, necessary for the purpose of maintaining international peace and security.

2. Such agreement or agreements shall govern the numbers and types of forces, their degree of readiness and general location, and the nature of the facilities and assistance to be provided.

3.   The agreement or agreements shall be negotiated as soon as possible on the initiative of the Security Council. They shall be concluded between the Security Council and Members or between the Security Council and groups of Members and shall be subject to ratification by the signatory states in accordance with their respective constitutional processes.

Article 44

When the Security Council has decided to use force it shall, before calling upon a Member not represented on it to provide armed forces in fulfilment of the obligations assumed under Article 43, invite that Member, if the Member so desires, to participate in the decisions of the Security Council concerning the employment of contingents of that Member's armed forces.

Article 45

In order to enable the United Nations to take urgent military measures, Members shall hold immediately available national air-force contingents for combined international enforcement action. The strength and degree of readiness of these contingents and plans for their combined action shall be determined within the limits laid down in the special agreement or agreements referred to in Article 43, by the Security Council with the assistance of the Military Staff Committee.

Article 46

Plans for the application of armed force shall be made by the Security Council with the assistance of the Military Staff Committee.

Article 47

1. There shall be established a Military Staff Committee to advise and assist the Security Council on all questions relating to the Security Council's military requirements for the maintenance of international peace and security, the employment and command of forces placed at its disposal, the regulation of armaments, and possible disarmament.

2. The Military Staff Committee shall consist of the Chiefs of Staff of the permanent members of the Security Council or their representatives. Any Member of the United Nations not permanently represented on the Committee shall be invited by the Committee to be associated with it when the efficient discharge of the Committee's responsibilities requires the participation of that Member in its work.

3. The Military Staff Committee shall be responsible under the Security Council for the strategic direction of any armed forces placed at the disposal of the Security Council. Questions relating to the command of such forces shall be worked out subsequently.

4. The Military Staff Committee, with the authorization of the Security Council and after consultation with appropriate regional agencies, may establish regional sub-committees.

Article 48

1. The action required to carry out the decisions of the Security Council for the maintenance of international peace and security shall be taken by all the Members

of the United Nations or by some of them, as the Security Council may determine.

2.   Such decisions shall be carried out by the Members of the United Nations directly and through their action in the appropriate international agencies of which they are members.

Article 49

The Members of the United Nations shall join in affording mutual assistance in carrying out the measures decided upon by the Security Council.

Article 50

If preventive or enforcement measures against any state are taken by the Security Council, any other state, whether a Member of the United Nations or not, which finds itself confronted with special economic problems arising from the carrying out of those measures shall have the right to consult the Security Council with regard to a solution of those problems.

Article 51

Nothing in the present Charter shall impair the inherent right of individual or collective self-defence if an armed attack occurs against a Member of the United Nations, until the Security Council has taken measures necessary to maintain international peace and security. Measures taken by Members in the exercise of this right of self-defence shall be immediately reported to the Security Council and shall not in any way affect the authority and responsibility of the Security Council under the present Charter to take at any time such action as it deems necessary in order to maintain or restore international peace and security.

Chapter VIII:
Regional Arrangements

Article 52

1. Nothing in the present Charter precludes the existence of regional arrangements or agencies for dealing with such matters relating to the maintenance of international peace and security as are appropriate for regional action provided that such arrangements or agencies and their activities are consistent with the Purposes and Principles of the United Nations.

2. The Members of the United Nations entering into such arrangements or constituting such agencies shall make every effort to achieve pacific settlement of local disputes through such regional arrangements or by such regional agencies before referring them to the Security Council.

3. The Security Council shall encourage the development of pacific settlement of local disputes through such regional arrangements or by such regional agencies either on the initiative of the states concerned or by reference from the Security Council.

4. This Article in no way impairs the application of Articles 34 and 35.

Article 53

1. The Security Council shall, where appropriate, utilize such regional arrangements or agencies for enforce-

ment action under its authority. But no enforcement action shall be taken under regional arrangements or by regional agencies without the authorization of the Security Council, with the exception of measures against any enemy state, as defined in paragraph 2 of this Article, provided for pursuant to Article 107 or in regional arrangements directed against renewal of aggressive policy on the part of any such state, until such time as the Organization may, on request of the Governments concerned, be charged with the responsibility for preventing further aggression by such a state.

2. The term enemy state as used in paragraph 1 of this Article applies to any state which during the Second World War has been an enemy of any signatory of the present Charter.

Article 54

The Security Council shall at all times be kept fully informed of activities undertaken or in contemplation under regional arrangements or by regional agencies for the maintenance of international peace and security. [...]

Chapter X:
The Economic and Social Council

[...]

Article 65

The Economic and Social Council may furnish information to the Security Council and shall assist the Security Council upon its request. [...]

Chapter XV:
The Secretariat

Article 97

The Secretariat shall comprise a Secretary-General and such staff as the Organization may require. The Secretary-General shall be appointed by the General Assembly upon the recommendation of the Security Council. He shall be the chief administrative officer of the Organization.

Article 98

The Secretary-General shall act in that capacity in all meetings of the General Assembly, of the Security Council, of the Economic and Social Council, and of the Trusteeship Council, and shall perform such other functions as are entrusted to him by these organs. The Secretary-General shall make an annual report to the General Assembly on the work of the Organization.

Article 99

The Secretary-General may bring to the attention of the Security Council any matter which in his opinion may threaten the maintenance of international peace and security. [...]

Chapter XVI:
Miscellaneous Provisions

[...]

Article 103

In the event of a conflict between the obligations of the Members of the United Nations under the present Charter and their obligations under any other international agreement, their obligations under the present Charter shall prevail. [...]

Chapter XVIII:
Amendments

Article 108

Amendments to the present Charter shall come into force for all Members of the United Nations when they have been adopted by a vote of two thirds of the members of the General Assembly and ratified in accordance with their respective constitutional processes by two thirds of the Members of the United Nations, including all the permanent members of the Security Council.

Article 109

1. A General Conference of the Members of the United Nations for the purpose of reviewing the present Charter may be held at a date and place to be fixed by a two-thirds vote of the members of the General Assembly and by a vote of any nine members of the Security Council. Each Member of the United Nations shall have one vote in the conference.

2. Any alteration of the present Charter recommended by a two-thirds vote of the conference shall take effect when ratified in accordance with their respective constitutional processes by two thirds of the Mem-

bers of the United Nations including all the permanent members of the Security Council.

3.   If such a conference has not been held before the tenth annual session of the General Assembly following the coming into force of the present Charter, the proposal to call such a conference shall be placed on the agenda of that session of the General Assembly, and the conference shall be held if so decided by a majority vote of the members of the General Assembly and by a vote of any seven members of the Security Council. [...]

Annex 2:
Provisional Rules of Procedure of the Security Council

S/96/Rev.7

Chapter I: Meetings

Rule 1

Meetings of the Security Council shall, with the exception of the periodic meetings referred to in rule 4, be held at the call of the President at any time he deems necessary, but the interval between meetings shall not exceed fourteen days.

Rule 2

The President shall call a meeting of the Security Council at the request of any member of the Security Council.

Rule 3

The President shall call a meeting of the Security Council if a dispute or situation is brought to the attention of the Security Council under Article 35 or under Article I I (3) of the Charter, or if the General Assembly makes recommendations or refers any question to the Security Council under Article 11 (2), or if the Secretary-General brings to the attention of the Security Council any matter under Article 99.

Rule 4

Periodic meetings of the Security Council called for in Article 28 (2) of the Charter shall be held twice a year, at such times as the Security Council may decide.

Rule 5

Meetings of the Security Council shall normally be held at the seat of the United Nations.

Any member of the Security-Council or the Secretary-General may propose that the Security Council should meet at another place. Should the Security Council accept any such proposal, it shall decide upon the place and the period during which the Council shall meet at such place.

Chapter II:
Agenda

Rule 6

The Secretary-General shall immediately bring to the attention of all representatives on the Security Council all communications from States, organs of the United Nations, or the Secretary-General concerning any matter for the consideration of the Security Council in accordance with the provisions of the Charter.

Rule 7

The provisional agenda for each meeting of the Security Council shall be drawn up by the Secretary-General and approved by the President of the Security Council.

Only items which have been brought to the attention of the representatives on the Security Council in accordance with rule 6, items covered by rule 10, or matters which the Security Council had previously decided to defer, may be included in the provisional agenda.

Rule 8

The provisional agenda for a meeting shall be communicated by the Secretary-General to the representatives on the Security Council at least three days before the meeting, but in urgent circumstances it may be communicated simultaneously with the notice of the meeting.

Rule 9

The first item of the provisional agenda for each meeting of the Security Council shall be the adoption of the agenda.

Rule 10

Any item of the agenda of a meeting of the Security Council, consideration of which has not been completed at that meeting, shall, unless the Security Council otherwise decides, automatically be included in the agenda of the next meeting.

Rule 11

The Secretary-General shall communicate each week to the representatives on the Security Council a summary statement of matters of which the Security Council is seized and of the stage reached in their consideration.

Rule 12

The provisional agenda for each periodic meeting shall be circulated to the members of the Security Council at least twenty-one days before the opening of the meeting. Any subsequent change in or addition to the provisional agenda shall be brought to the notice of the members at least five days before the meeting. The Security Council may, however, in urgent circumstances, make additions to the agenda at any time during a periodic meeting.

The provisions of rule 7, paragraph 1, and of rule 9, shall apply also to periodic meetings.

Chapter III:
Representation and Credentials

Rule 13

Each member of the Security Council shall be represented at the meetings of the Security Council by an accredited representative. The credentials of a representative on the Security Council shall be communicated to the Secretary-General not less than twenty-four hours before he takes his seat on the Security Council. The credentials shall be issued either by the Head of the State or of the Government concerned or by its Minister of Foreign Affairs. The Head of Government or Minister of Foreign Affairs of each member of the Security Council shall be entitled to sit on the Security Council without submitting credentials.

Rule 14

Any Member of the United Nations not a member of the Security Council and any State not a Member of the United Nations, if invited to participate in a meeting or meetings of the Security Council, shall submit credentials for the representative appointed by it for this purpose. The credentials of such a representative shall be communicated to the Secretary-General not less than twenty-four hours before the first meeting which he is invited to attend.

Rule 15

The credentials of representatives on the Security Council and of any representative appointed in accordance with rule 14 shall he examined by the Secretary-General who shall submit a report to the Security Council for approval.

Rule 16

Pending the approval of the credentials of a representative on the Security Council in accordance with rule 15, such representative shall be seated provisionally with the same rights as other representatives.

Rule 17

Any representative on the Security Council, to whose credentials objection has been made within the Security Council, shall continue to sit with the same rights as other representatives until the Security Council has decided the matter.

Chapter IV:
Presidency

Rule 18

The presidency of the Security Council shall be held in turn by the members of the Security Council in the English alphabetical order of their names. Each President shall hold office for one calendar month.

Rule 19

The President shall preside over the meetings of the Security Council and, under the authority of the Security Council, shall represent it in its capacity as an organ of the United Nations.

Rule 20

Whenever the President of the Security Council deems that for the proper fulfillment of the responsibilities of the presidency he should not preside over the Council during the consideration of a particular question with which the member he represents is directly connected, he shall indicate his decision to the Council. The presidential chair shall then devolve, for the purpose of the consideration of that question, on the representative of the member next in English alphabetical order, it being understood that the provisions of this rule shall apply to the representatives on the Security Council called upon successively to preside. This rule shall not affect the representative capacity of the President as stated in rule 19, or his duties under rule 7.

Chapter V:
Secretariat

Rule 21

The Secretary-General shall act in that capacity in all meetings of the Security Council. The Secretary-General may authorize a deputy to act in his place at meetings of the Security Council.

Rule 22

The Secretary-General, or his deputy acting on his behalf, may make either oral or written statements to the Security Council concerning any question under consideration by it.

Rule 23

The Secretary-General may be appointed by the Security Council, in accordance with rule 28, as rapporteur for a specified question.

Rule 24

The Secretary-General shall provide the staff required by the Security Council. This staff shall form a part of the Secretariat.

Rule 25

The Secretary-General shall give to representatives on the Security Council notice of meetings of the Security Council and of its commissions and committees.

Rule 26

The Secretary-General shall be responsible for the preparation of documents required by the Security Council and shall, except in urgent circumstances, distribute them at least forty-eight hours in advance of the meeting at which they are to be considered.

Chapter VI:
Conduct of Business

Rule 27

The President shall call upon representatives in the order in which they signify their desire to speak.

Rule 28

The Security Council may appoint a commission or committee or a rapporteur for a specified question.

Rule 29

The President may accord precedence to any rapporteur appointed by the Security Council.

The Chairman of a commission or committee, or the rapporteur appointed by the commission or committee to present its report, may be accorded precedence for the purpose of explaining the report.

Rule 30

If a representative raises a point of order, the President shall immediately state his ruling. If it is challenged, the President shall submit his ruling to the Security Council for immediate decision and it shall stand unless overruled.

Rule 31

Proposed resolutions, amendments and substantive motions shall normally be placed before the representatives in writing.

Rule 32

Principal motions and draft resolutions shall have precedence in the order of their submission.

Parts of a motion or of a draft resolution shall be voted on separately at the request of any representative, unless the original mover objects.

Rule 33

The following motions shall have precedence in the order named over all principal motions and draft resolutions relative to the subject before the meeting:

1. To suspend the meeting;
2. To adjourn the meeting;
3. To adjourn the meeting to a certain day or hour;
4. To refer any matter to a committee, to the Secretary-General or to a rapporteur;
5. To postpone discussion of the question to a certain day or indefinitely; or
6. To introduce an amendment.

Any motion for the suspension or for the simple adjournment of the meeting shall be decided without debate.

Rule 34

It shall not be necessary for any motion or draft resolution proposed by a representative on the Security Council to be seconded before being put to a vote.

Rule 35

A motion or draft resolution can at any time be withdrawn so long as no vote has been taken with respect to it.

If the motion or draft resolution has been seconded, the representative on the Security Council who has seconded it may require that it be put to the vote as his motion or draft resolution with the same right of precedence as if the original mover had not withdrawn it.

Rule 36

If two or more amendments to a motion or draft resolution are proposed, the President shall rule on the order in which they are to be voted upon. Ordinarily, the Security Council shall first vote on the amendment furthest removed in substance from the original proposal and then on the amendment next furthest removed until all amendments have been put to the vote, but when an amendment adds to or deletes from the text of a motion or draft resolution, that amendment shall be voted on first.

Rule 37

Any Member of the United Nations which is not a member of the Security Council may be invited, as the result of a decision of the Security Council, to participate, without vote, in the discussion of any question brought before the Security Council when the Security Council considers that the interests of that Member are specially affected, or when a Member brings a matter to the attention of the Security Council in accordance with Article 35 (1) of the Charter.

Rule 38

Any Member of the United Nations invited in accordance with the preceding rule, or in application of Article 32 of the Charter, to participate in the discussions of the Security Council may submit proposals and draft resolutions.

These proposals and draft resolutions may be put to a vote only at the request of a representative on the Security Council.

Rule 39

The Security Council may invite members of the Secretariat or other persons, whom it considers competent for the purpose, to supply it with information or to give other assistance in examining matters within its competence.

Chapter VII:
Voting

Rule 40

Voting in the Security Council shall be in accordance with the relevant Articles of the Charter and of the Statute of the International Court of Justice

Chapter VIII:
Languages

Rule 41

Arabic, Chinese, English, French, Russian and Spanish shall be both the official and the working languages of the Security Council.

Rule 42

Speeches made in any of the six languages of the Security Council shall be interpreted into the other five languages.

Rule 43

[Deleted]

Rule 44

Any representative may make a speech in a language other than the languages of the Security Council. In this case, he shall himself provide for interpretation into one of those languages. Interpretation into the other languages of the Security Council by the interpreters of the Secretariat may be based on the interpretation given in the first such language.

Rule 45

Verbatim records of meetings of the Security Council shall be drawn up in the languages of the Council.

Rule 46

All resolutions and other documents shall be published in the languages of the Security Council.

Rule 47

Documents of the Security Council shall, if the Security Council so decides, be published in any language other than the languages of the Council.

Chapter IX:
Publicity of Meetings, Records

Rule 48

Unless it decides otherwise, the Security Council shall meet in public. Any recommendation to the General Assembly regarding the appointment of the Secretary-General shall be discussed and decided at a private meeting.

Rule 49

Subject to the provisions of rule 51, the verbatim record of each meeting of the Security Council shall be made available to the representatives on the Security Council and to the representatives of any other States which have participated in the meeting not later than 10 a.m. of the first working day following the meeting.

Rule 50

The representatives of the States which have participated in the meeting shall, within two working days after the time indicated in rule 49, inform the Secretary-General of any corrections they wish to have made in the verbatim record.

Rule 51

The Security Council may decide that for a private meeting the record shall be made in a single copy alone. This record shall be kept by the Secretary-General. The representatives of the States which have participated in the meeting shall, within a period of ten days, inform the Secretary-General of any corrections they wish to have made in this record.

Rule 52

Corrections that have been requested shall be considered approved unless the President is of the opinion that they are sufficiently important to be submitted to the representatives on the Security Council. In the latter case, the representatives on the Security Council shall submit within two working days any comments they may wish to make. In the absence of objections in this period of time, the record shall be corrected as requested.

Rule 53

The verbatim record referred to in rule 49 or the record referred to in rule 51, in which no corrections have been requested in the period of time required by rules 50 and 51, respectively, or which has been corrected in accordance with the provisions of rule 52, shall be considered as approved. It shall be signed by the President and shall become the official record of the Security Council.

Rule 54

The official record of public meetings of the Security Council, as well as the documents annexed thereto, shall be published in the official languages as soon as possible.

Rule 55

At the close of each private meeting the Security Council shall issue a *communiqué* through the Secretary-General.

Rule 56

The representatives of the Members of the United Nations which have taken part in a private meeting shall at all times have the right to consult the record of that meeting in the office of the Secretary-General. The Security Council may at any time grant access to this record to authorized representatives of other Members of the United Nations.

Rule 57

The Secretary-General shall, once each year, submit to the Security Council a list of the records and documents which up to that time have been considered confidential. The Security Council shall decide which of these shall be made available to other Members of the United Nations, which shall be made public, and which shall continue to remain confidential.

Chapter X:
Admission of New Members

Rule 58

Any State which desires to become a Member of the United Nations shall submit an application to the Secretary-General. This application shall contain a declaration made in a formal instrument that it accepts the obligations contained in the Charter.

Rule 59

The Secretary-General shall immediately place the application for membership before the representatives on the Security Council. Unless the Security Council decides otherwise, the application shall be referred by the President to a committee of the Security Council upon which each member of the Security Council shall be represented. The committee shall examine any application referred to it and report its conclusions thereon to the Council not less than thirty-five days in advance of a regular session of the General Assembly or, if a special session of the General Assembly is called, not less than fourteen days in advance of such session.

Rule 60

The Security Council shall decide whether in its judgement the applicant is a peace-loving State and is able and willing to carry out the obligations contained in the Charter and, accordingly, whether to recommend the applicant State for membership.

If the Security Council recommends the applicant State for membership, it shall forward to the General Assembly the recommendation with a complete record of the discussion.

If the Security Council does not recommend the applicant State for membership or postpones the consideration of the application, it shall submit a special report to the General Assembly with a complete record of the discussion.

In order to ensure the consideration of its recommendation at the next session of the General Assembly following the receipt of the application, the Security Council shall make its recommendation not less than twenty-five days in advance of a regular session of the General Assembly, nor less than four days in advance of a special session.

In special circumstances, the Security Council may decide to make a recommendation to the General Assembly concerning an application for membership subsequent to the expiration of the time limits set forth in the preceding paragraph.

Chapter XI:
Relations with Other United Nations Organs

Rule 61

Any meeting of the Security Council held in pursuance of the Statute of the International Court of Justice for the purpose of the election of members of the Court shall continue until as many candidates as are required for all the seats to be filled have obtained in one or more ballots an absolute majority of votes.

Appendix
Provisional Procedure for Dealing with Communications from Private Individuals and Non-Governmental Bodies

A. A list of all communications from private individuals and non-governmental bodies relating to matters of which the Security Council is seized shall be circulated to all representatives on the Security Council.

B. A copy of any communication on the list shall be given by the Secretariat to any representative on the Security Council at his request.

Annex 3:
Documents

Security Council Press Statement on adoption of revised 507 Note (S/2010/507), 26 July 2010

The following Security Council press statement was read out by Council President U. Joy Ogwu (Nigeria):

This morning, the Security Council adopted a note by the President concerning the improvement of the working methods of the Council. The note is the product of intensive work on the part of the Security Council's Informal Working Group on Documentation and Other Procedural Questions over the past several months. It builds on previous Council efforts to document its working methods, enhance its efficiency and transparency as well as interaction and dialogue with non-Council members by updating presidential note 507, adopted in 2006 (document S/2006/507). Members of the Council have been actively engaged in these efforts, and the open debate in April on this issue made an important contribution to the revision of note 507.

Some of the new elements include the following measures:

* The revised note incorporates the Council's agreements in two other presidential notes (documents S/2007/749 and S/2008/847) on the working methods of the Council adopted after issuance of note 507

* There is a new section on planning and reporting for Security Council missions (see Chapter XI[1])

---

[1] Chapter XI of S/2010/507

- The members of the Council express their intention to maintain regular communication with the Peace-building Commission, which had not been mentioned in previous Council notes on its working methods (see paragraph 61)

- It refers as well for the first time to the use of informal dialogues by the Council in recent years (see paragraph 59)

- Its intention to enhance its dialogue with troop-contributing countries to peacekeeping, especially before it considers peacekeeping operation mandate renewals (see paragraph 33)

- It clarifies expectations on the part of both the Council and Secretariat for the submission of Secretary-General reports and briefings (see paragraphs 14, 16, 21 and 22)

The members of the Security Council will continue to consider ways to improve the working methods of the Council, including through the Informal Working Group on Documentation and Other Procedural Questions.

Background Note on the "Arria-Formula" Meetings of the Security Council Members

INFORMAL NON-PAPER[1]

25 October 2002

The "Arria-formula meetings" are a relatively recent practice of the members of the Security Council. Like the informal consultations of the whole of the Security Council, they are not envisaged in the Charter of the United Nations or the Security Council's provisional rules of procedure. Under Article 30 of the Charter, however, the Council is the master of its own procedure and has the latitude to determine its own practices.

The "Arria-formula meetings" are very informal, confidential gatherings which enable Security Council members to have a frank and private exchange of views, within a flexible procedural framework, with persons whom the inviting member or members of the Council (who also act as the facilitators or convenors) believe it would be beneficial to hear and/or to whom they may wish to convey a message. They provide interested Council members an opportunity to engage in a direct dialogue with high representatives of Governments and international organizations – often at the latter's request – as well as non-State parties, on matters with which they are concerned and which fall within the purview of responsibility of the Security Council.

---

[1] Prepared by the United Nations Secretariat.

The process is named after Ambassador Diego Arria of Venezuela, who, as the representative of Venezuela on the Council (1992-1993), initiated the practice in 1992. Although Ambassador Arria, as the then President of the Security Council, had himself convened in 1992 as an "Arria-formula meeting", the recent practice suggests a preference for such initiatives to be taken by members of the Council other than the President. The convening member is also chairing such meetings.

The "Arria-formula meetings" differ from the consultations of the whole of the Council in the following respects:

- Such informal gatherings do not constitute an activity of the Council and are convened at the initiative of a member or members of the Council. Participation in such meetings is for individual members to decide upon and there have been instances when some members chose not to attend.

- They are held in a Conference Room, and not in the Security Council Consultation Room.

- The convenor issues a written invitation to the other fourteen members, indicating the place, date and time of the "Arria-formula meeting", as well as the name of the party to be heard, by a fax from his/her Mission rather than by notification from the Secretariat.

- They are not announced in the daily Journal of the United Nations.

- Unless so invited, members of the Secretariat are not expected to attend, except for interpreters and a Conference Officer.

"Arria-formula" meetings[1]

The following elements appear to represent the common understanding of the Informal Working Group on Documentation and Other Procedural Questions on "Arria-formula" meetings.

- The members of the Security Council are encouraged to plan "Arria-formula" meetings, in accordance with paragraph 54 of the Note by the President of the Security Council (S/2006/507), and to take part in such meetings.

- The content of the background note on "Arria-formula" meetings, prepared by the Secretariat in 2002, provides a useful description of current and past practice of "Arria-formula" meetings, and the members are encouraged to utilize the background note as a guideline without undermining the flexibility of "Arria-formula" meetings.

- Any member of the Security Council convening an "Arria-formula" meeting is encouraged to carefully organize the meeting, so as to maintain its informal character.

- Any member of the Security Council convening an "Arria-formula" meeting should inform all participating Security Council members about the planned procedure for and participants in the meeting, and is encouraged to do so well in advance.

---

[1] Prepared by the Chairman of the Working Group on Documentation and Other Procedural Questions. The content of this document was reported orally to the Security Council on 20 December 2006.

Informal interactive dialogues and other informal meetings of the Security Council

DATE / VENUE	DESCRIPTIVE NAME	SUBJECT	BRIEFER	NON- SC / NON- UN PARTICIPANTS	LISTED IN JOURNAL	LISTED IN SC PROGRAMME OF WORK	LISTED IN ANNUAL REPORT
19 July 2011	Informal interactive dialogue	Eritrea		Eritrea, Djibouti, Ethiopia, Somalia, Kenya, Uganda, Inter-governmental Authority on Development Facilitator for Somalia	NO		
22 June 2011	Informal interactive dialogue	Darfur	Joint African Union-UN Chief Mediator for Dar-fur, Minister of State for Foreign Affairs of Qatar		NO		
15 June 2011	Informal interactive dialogue	Libya		Minister of Communications designate of Uganda, Minister for Foreign Affairs and Coop-eration of Mauritania	NO		

DATE / VENUE	DESCRIPTIVE NAME	SUBJECT	BRIEFER	NON- SC / NON- UN PARTICIPANTS	LISTED IN JOURNAL	LISTED IN SC PROGRAMME OF WORK	LISTED IN ANNUAL REPORT
2 February 2011	Informal interactive dialogue	Burundi	Representative of the Secretary-General in Burundi and Head of the United Nations Office in Burundi (BNUB), Chair of the Country-specific Configuration of the Peacebuilding Commission for Burundi	Burundi	NO		
10 December 2010	Informal interactive discussion	Liberia	SRSG Loj, Chair of the Country-specific Configuration for Liberia of the Peacebuilding Commission	Liberia	NO		
21 October 2010	Informal interactive discussion	MINURCAT	Chad	Chad, Special Representative of President Déby for MINURCAT and Head of the CONAFIT (Coordination nationale d'appui au déploiement de la Force internationale à l'Est du Tchad	NO		

DATE / VENUE	DESCRIPTIVE NAME	SUBJECT	BRIEFER	NON-SC / NON-UN PARTICIPANTS	LISTED IN JOURNAL	LISTED IN SC PROGRAMME OF WORK	LISTED IN ANNUAL REPORT
9 August 2010	Informal interactive discussion	Central African Republic	Minister of Foreign Affairs of the Central African Republic, Chair of the Country-specific Configuration of the Peacebuilding Commission for the Central African Republic	Minister of Foreign Affairs of the Central African Republic	NO		
14 June 2010	Informal interactive discussion	Republic of Korea / Democratic People's Republic of Korea ("Cheonan incident")	Republic of Korea, Democratic People's Republic of Korea	Republic of Korea, Democratic People's Republic of Korea	NO		YES
20 May 2010	Informal interactive discussion	MINURCAT	Chad	Chad, Special Representative of President Déby for MINURCAT and Head of the CONAFIT (Coordination nationale d'appui au déploiement de la Force internationale à l'Est du Tchad	NO		NO
5 May 2010	Informal interactive discussion	MINURCAT	Special Representative of the Secretary-General Mahmoud	Chad, CAR	NO		NO

83

DATE / VENUE	DESCRIPTIVE NAME	SUBJECT	BRIEFER	NON-SC / NON-UN PARTICIPANTS	LISTED IN JOURNAL	LISTED IN SC PROGRAMME OF WORK	LISTED IN ANNUAL REPORT
22 March 2010 Conf. Rm. 5	Informal interactive discussion	MINURCAT	Under-Secretary-General for Peacekeeping Operations	Chad, CAR	NO		NO
5 June 2009 Conf. Rm. 6	Informal interactive discussion	Sri Lanka	Secretary-General	Sri Lanka	NO		YES
30 April 2009 Conf. Rm. 7	Informal interactive discussion	Sri Lanka (humanitarian situation)	Under-Secretary-General John Holmes	Sri Lanka	NO		YES
22 April 2009 Conf. Rm. 6	Informal interactive discussion	Sri Lanka (humanitarian situation)	Chef de Cabinet Vijay Nambiar	Sri Lanka	NO		YES
26 March 2009 Conf. Rm. 7	Informal interactive discussion	Sri Lanka (humanitarian situation)	Under-Secretary-General John Holmes	Sri Lanka	NO		YES
12 February 2009	Informal interactive discussion	Darfur	African Union-Arab League delegation	Joint delegation from the African Union and League of Arab States	NO		YES

DATE / VENUE	DESCRIPTIVE NAME	SUBJECT	BRIEFER	NON- SC / NON- UN PARTICIPANTS	LISTED IN JOURNAL	LISTED IN SC PROGRAMME OF WORK	LISTED IN ANNUAL REPORT
17 April 2008	Meeting between the members of the UN Security Council and the members of the African Union Peace and Security Council	Cooperation between the UNSC and the African Union Peace and Security Council	Permanent Representative of Ethiopia to the African Union and the African Union Peace and Security Council Chair for the Month of April, Sahle-Work Zewde	African Union Peace and Security Council at ambassadorial level	NO* (The Journal lists a joint briefing for the SC and GA)		YES* (The report does not describe meeting as including GA)
26 February 2008 Conf. Rm. 7	Informal interactive discussion	Chad/Sudan	Minister for Foreign Affairs of Chad, Ahmad Allam-Mi	Minister for Foreign Affairs of Chad	NO		NO
13 July 2007	Informal dialogue	Sudan	African Union Commission Chairperson Alpha Oumar Konaré	African Union Commission Chairperson	NO		NO
9 July 2007	Informal dialogue	Kosovo	Lieutenant-General Roland Kather, Commander of KFOR	Commander of KFOR			NO
27 April 2007 Conf. Rm 8	Informal meeting	Somalia	Minister for Foreign Affairs of Ethiopia, Seum Mesfin	Minister for Foreign Affairs of Ethiopia	NO		NO

DATE / VENUE	DESCRIPTIVE NAME	SUBJECT	BRIEFER	NON- SC / NON- UN PARTICIPANTS	LISTED IN JOURNAL	LISTED IN SC PROGRAMME OF WORK	LISTED IN ANNUAL REPORT
24 April 2007	Informal private discussion	Somalia	Permanent Observer of the African Union, Lila Hanitra Ratsifandriha-manana, Assistant-Secretary-General for Political Affairs Tuliameni Kalomoh, Under-Secretary-General for Humanitarian Affairs and Emergency Relief Coordinator John Holmes, Director of Africa Division, Department of Peacekeeping Operations, Dmitry Titov	Permanent Observer of the African Union	NO		YES
16 April 2007	Informal private discussion	Sudan	Secretary-General, African Union Commission Chairperson Konaré, African Union Commissioner for Peace and Security, Said Djinnit, United Nations Special Representative Jan Eliasson, African Union Special Representative Salim Ahmed Salim	Secretary-General, African Union Commission Chairperson, African Union Commissioner for Peace and Security, UN and African Union special representatives to Sudan			NO

DATE / VENUE	DESCRIPTIVE NAME	SUBJECT	BRIEFER	NON-SC / NON-UN PARTICIPANTS	LISTED IN JOURNAL	LISTED IN SC PROGRAMME OF WORK	LISTED IN ANNUAL REPORT
22 March 2007	Informal private meeting	Chad / Sudan	Minister for Foreign Affairs of Chad, Ahmad Allam-Mi, Colonel Idriss Dokomy Adiker of Chad	Minister for Foreign Affairs of Chad, Military officer of Chad	NO		NO
6 February 2006 SC Chamber	Informal event / Meeting between SC members and US Senators Lugar, Voinovich and Coleman	Non-proliferation issues	Senator Richard Lugar, Chairman of the Senate Foreign Relations Committee, and other members of the United States Senate	Chairman of the US Senate Foreign Relations Committee and other Senators			YES
20 January 2000 SC Chamber	Special meeting	Relationship between the UN and the USA; the Helms-Biden Law	Chairman of the United States Senate Committee on Foreign Relations, Jesse Helms	Chairman of the United States Senate Committee on Foreign Relations			
3 April 1996 SC Chamber	Informal meeting	General discussion of SC issues, in connection with the visit of the President of Italy to the UN	President of Italy, Dr. Oscar Luigi Scalfaro	President of Italy			

Formats of Meetings¹ Related to the Security Council

Names of Meetings			Participation of Non-Council Members² in the Discussion	Briefing by the Secretariat	Official Records	Venue
Meetings of the Security Council (*para.* 36 of the Note)	Public meetings	Open debate	Non-Council members may be invited to participate in the discussion upon their request	May be conducted	Published	Security Council Chamber
		Debate	Non-Council members that are directly concerned or affected or have special interest in the matter under consideration may be invited to participate in the discussion upon their request	May be conducted		Security Council Chamber
		Briefing	Only Council members may deliver statements following briefings	Conducted		
		Adoption	Non-Council members may or may not be invited to participate in the discussion upon their request	Not conducted		
	Private meetings³	Private meeting	Non-Council members may be invited to participate in the discussion upon their request	May be conducted	Made in a single copy only and kept by the Secretary General	Security Council Chamber
		TCC meeting	Parties prescribed in resolution 1353 (2001) are invited to participate in the discussion, in accordance with the resolution	May be conducted		ECOSOC/TC Chamber or Conference Room
Meetings of Members of the Security Council	Informal consultations of the whole (*para.* 20 to 27 of the Note)		Non-Council members not invited	May be conducted	Not made	SC Consultations Room
Informal Dialogue (*para.* 59 of the Note)			By invitation only	May or may not be conducted	Not made	Conference Room
"Arria-formula" meeting (*para.* 65 of the Note)			By invitation only	Usually not conducted	Not made	Conference Room or Permanent Mission of an SC member

Notes:

1. Only those which appear in the Note by the President of the Security Council (S/2010/507) are shown on this table.

2. Any Member State of the United Nations which is not a member of the Security Council, whether participating at its own request or invited by the Council, is invited to formal meetings of the Council pursuant to rule 37 of the Provisional Rules of Procedure. Members of the Secretariat or other persons participating in a formal Council meeting are invited pursuant to rule 39.

3. Closed to the public. Member States of the United Nations which are not a member of the Security Council may be invited to be present.

Major Types of Actions Taken by the Security Council[1]

Types of actions Document Symbol	Usual decision procedure
Resolution S/RES/[number] ([year])	An affirmative vote of nine members including the concurrent votes of the P5 in a public meeting (Adoption).
Statement by the President S/PRST/[year]/[number]	Consensus in informal consultations or by "no objection" procedure. The President of the Security Council reads out the statement in a public meeting (Adoption).
Note by the President	Consensus in informal consultations or by "no objection" procedure.
Letter from the President[2]	
Press statement	Consensus. The President of the Security Council reads out the statement to the press.

---

1 The content of this table is neither officially prescribed nor intended to covers all actions by the Security Council.
2 In some exceptional cases, the letter is adopted in a public meeting (Adoption).

SECURITY COUNCIL HANDBOOK GLOSSARY[1]

Agenda

The programme of work adopted by the Security Council at the start of each meeting. Unlike most UN organs, the Council does not adopt an "agenda" listing multiple items which it intends to consider.

Annual Report of the Security Council to the General Assembly

Submitted to the General Assembly each year pursuant to Art. 15(1) and Art. 24(3) of the UN Charter. With a reporting period of 1 Aug. to 31 July of the following year, the report is drafted in accordance with Section XII of S/2010/507.

Briefer

Individuals, often representing the Secretary-General or other parts of the UN system, who give an oral presentation to Council members on a matter under their consideration

Communiqué

Pursuant to rule 55 of the Council's provisional rules of procedure, a communiqué is issued at the close of each private meeting.

Consultations (of the whole) / "informal consultations"

"Consultations of the whole" are consultations held in private with all 15 Council members present. Such consultations are held in the Consultations Room, are announced in the UN Journal, have an agreed agenda and interpretation, and may involve one or more briefers. The consultations are closed to non-Council Member States. "Informal consultations" mostly refer to "consultations of the whole", but in different contexts may also refer to consultations among the 15 Council members or only some of them held without a Journal announcement and interpretation.

---

1 The glossary has been compiled for information purposes only and the descriptions contained therein are not official definitions.

Credentials

In addition to the general credentials submitted by each UN Member State, in order to be accredited to participate in the Security Council, the Head of State or Government or the Minister for Foreign Affairs of each Security Council member must submit credentials specific to the Council for every representative of its delegation.

Distribution of documents

All official documents of the Security Council, which include the decisions of the Council, reports of the Secretary-General to the Council, letters sent by the Council President, and communications sent to the Council, are distributed to all UN Member States on a daily basis.

Elected members ("non-permanent members")

Pursuant to Article 23 of the UN Charter, ten of the 15 Council members are elected by the General Assembly for two-year terms on the Security Council.

Expert groups

Groups of experts, appointed in their individual capacities by the Secretary-General upon the request of the Security Council, to provide fact-finding information in connection with the work of the sanctions committees and counter-terrorism committees of the Security Council.

Group of friends

A number of Member States, which can include both Council members and non-Council Member States, which is self-organized to take the lead in connection with a specific item on the agenda of the Security Council.

Informal dialogues

An informal private meeting of the Security Council members convened in order to hold an off-the-record discussion with one or more non-Council Member States. The informal dialogues are presided over by the Council President and take place in a meeting room other than the Council Chamber or Consultations Room.

Informal Working Group of the Security Council on Documentation and Other Procedural Questions ("IWG")

Established in 1993 by the Security Council, the Informal Working Group meets, as necessary, to consider the working methods and procedures of the Security Council and to make recommendations for adoption by the Council as appropriate. The document S/2010/507 was drafted and agreed through the work of the Informal Working Group.

Journal of the United Nations

A calendar of UN meetings, agendas and events in New York which is issued daily.

Mandate

In the context of the document S/2010/507, the term "mandate" refers to the length of time and the governing principles under which such entities as UN peacekeeping forces, assistance missions or offices, representatives of the Secretary-General, or groups of experts have been authorized to perform tasks assigned by the Security Council.

Member States of the United Nations

States which are members of the United Nations Organization, and thereby have accepted all the obligations contained in the UN Charter.

Military Staff Committee

Under Articles 45, 46 and 47 of the UN Charter, the Military Staff Committee is to advise and assist the Security Council on all questions relating to the Security Council's military requirements for the maintenance of international peace and security.

Missions of the Security Council

Travel by some or all 15 members of the Security Council to regions related to matters under consideration by the Council.

Monthly assessment

A report written by each month's outgoing Council President, in his/her national capacity, summarizing the work of the Council during that Presidency.

Non-members

Member States of the United Nations which are neither permanent nor elected members of the Security Council.

Non-State actors

Individuals or groups which are non-governmental and which are relevant to matters under the consideration of the Security Council.

Note by the President

A document published in the name of the Council President on behalf of all 15 members of the Council which most often sets out decisions by the Council concerning its working methods and procedures.

Note by the President of the Security Council dated 26 July 2010 (S/2010/507)

A document (contained in this book) which was adopted by the members of the Security Council on 26 July 2010 in order to set out a list of recent practices and newly agreed working methods and procedures of the Council.

Official languages

The official languages of the Security Council are Arabic, Chinese, English, French, Russian and Spanish.

Open meeting

A meeting of the Security Council which can be attended by non-Council Member States and other individuals and for which there is a verbatim record and media coverage.

Peacebuilding Commission country-specific configuration

A subsidiary body of the Peacebuilding Commission (a body jointly created by the General Assembly and the Security Council) established in order to assist a specific country in post-conflict peace consolidation.

Peacekeeping missions

UN peacekeeping missions are mandated by the Security Council to provide security and political and peacebuilding support to countries in conflict or post-conflict situations. They are guided by the principles of consent of the host country, impartiality, and non-use of force except in self-defence, defence of the mandate, or protection of civilians if so authorized by the Council.

Permanent observers to the United Nations

Permanent Observers are representatives of entities other than Member States who have been accorded certain specified rights and who can be invited by the Council to participate in certain Council meetings.

Police-contributing countries

Countries contributing police personnel to UN peacekeeping or assistance missions or offices.

President of the Security Council

Under rule 18 of the Security Council's provisional rules of procedure, the presidency of the Council is held in turn by the members of the Council in English alphabetical order for a one-calendar-month period. Under rule 19, the President presides over the meetings of the Security Council and, under the authority of the Council, represents it in its capacity as a UN organ.

Principal organs of the United Nations

The Charter established six principal organs of the United Nations: the General Assembly, the Security Council, the Economic and Social Council, the Trusteeship Council, the International Court of Justice, and the Secretariat. The United Nations family, however, is much larger, encompassing 15 agencies and several programmes and bodies.

Programme of work ("calendar")

The Council agrees on both a monthly and a daily Programme of work. The monthly programme, or "calendar", initially agreed by the 15 members at the beginning of each presidency, sets out all agreed Council meetings and consultations for the month and can be amended by the members as the presidency progresses. The daily Programme of work is published in the (daily) UN Journal and indicates any meetings and consultations to be convened on that particular day together with their subjects.

Provisional rules of procedure of the Security Council

The provisional rules of procedure of the Security Council, last amended in 1982, set out the procedures, inter alia, for conducting meetings, representation and credentials, the presidency, conduct of business, voting, publicity and records of meetings, the admission of new UN Member States, and relations with other UN organs.

Reports of the Secretary-General

Reports submitted by the Secretary-General to the members of the Security Council on matters under consideration by the Council. The reports are usually, but not always, requested by the Council through a formal decision and issued as an official document of the Security Council. It is customary for the Secretary-General or a representative of the Secretary-General to present each report to the members of the Council either in a formal meeting or in closed consultations of the whole.

Representatives of the Secretary-General

The Secretary-General can appoint representatives and, if their work relates to the work of the Security Council, the appointment is usually confirmed in an exchange of letters between the Secretary-General and the Council President writing on behalf of the members. The representatives have various titles, including Special Representative, Special Envoy and Special Advisor, and they may serve as the head of a peacekeeping mission or of an assistance or political office, or represent the Secretary-General in negotiations.

Resolution 1353 (2001)

A resolution adopted by the Security Council in 2001 which sets out various provisions for improving communication and collaboration with countries contributing troops and/or police to missions established by the Security Council.

Resolution 1631 (2005)

A resolution adopted by the Security Council in 2005 on cooperation between the United Nations and regional and subregional organizations in the maintenance of international peace and security.

Sanctions committee

A subsidiary organ on which all 15 Security Council members are represented and which is established by the Council in order to carry out its directives in connection with sanctions regimes, which can include arms embargos, travel bans, freezing of accounts, and restrictions on the exploitation of natural resources.

Secretariat / Secretary-General

Composed of international staff and headed by the Secretary-General, the Secretariat is the principal organ established by the UN Charter which carries out the diverse day-to-day work of the Organization, including servicing the other principal organs and administering the programmes and policies decided by them.

Security Council

One of the principal organs of the UN, the Security Council has primary responsibility under the UN Charter for the maintenance of international peace and security.

Security Council Affairs Division of the Department of Political Affairs

The office in the UN Secretariat of which the principal function is to directly assist the Security Council with its work.

Speakers list

A list maintained by the Council President setting out, in order, all those Council members, non-Council Member States and individuals who will be making a statement during a Council meeting.

Spokesperson for the Secretary-General

The United Nations official responsible for the relations between the Secretariat and the press and who liaises with the Security Council Affairs Division in order to bring information concerning the Council and its work to the attention of journalists.

Statements by the President of the Security Council ("PRST")

A statement made by the President of the Security Council on behalf of the Council, adopted at a formal meeting of the Council and issued as an official document of the Council.

Statements to the press

A statement to the media made by the President of the Security Council on behalf of all 15 members and which is issued as a UN press release in English and French.

Subsidiary body

A committee or working group or other small entity created by the Security Council to carry out specific responsibilities under its direction.

Summary statement of matters of which the Security Council is seized

A document, updated each week, issued by the Secretary-General pursuant to rule 11 of the Council's provisional rules of procedure and which lists all matters relating to the Council's mandate for the maintenance of international peace and security which the Council has taken up in one or more formal meetings and of which the Council has not yet determined that it has completed its consideration.

Troop-contributing countries

Countries contributing troops to UN peacekeeping or assistance missions or offices.

UN Resident Coordinators

Under the aegis of the United Nations Development Programme (UNDP), a Resident Coordinator leads a United Nations country team (UNCT) and is the designated representative of the Secretary-General for development operations.

Verbatim record

A full transcript, published as an official Security Council document in all six official languages, of all statements made during a public meeting of the Council. For private meetings of the Council, the verbatim record is not issued as a published document, but is rather available for consultation only upon request.

Working Group of the Security Council on Peacekeeping Operations

A subsidiary body of the Security Council which meets, as necessary, to consider matters relating to peacekeeping operations mandated by the Council.